ARM YOURSELVES

WITH THE MIND OF CHRIST

Jan Grace

Jan Grace

ARM YOURSELVES - WITH THE MIND OF CHRIST

Copyright © 2015 by Jan Grace. All rights reserved.

No part of this publication may be reproduced, stored in a retrieval system or transmitted in any way by any means, electronic, mechanical, photocopy, recording or otherwise without the prior permission of the author except as provided by USA copyright law.

Unless otherwise noted, all scripture is taken from the King James Version of the Bible.

Scripture quotations marked (NKJV) are taken from the *New King James Version*. Copyright © 1982 by Thomas Nelson, Inc. Used by permission. All rights reserved.

Scripture quotations marked (NLT) are taken from the Holy Bible, *New Living Translation*, copyright © 1996. Used by permission of Tyndale House Publishers, Inc., Wheaton, Illinois 60189. All rights reserved.

Scripture quotations marked (ESV) are taken from The Holy Bible, *English Standard Version*. ©2001 by Crossway Bibles, a division of Good News Publishers. Used by permission. All rights reserved.

Scripture quotations marked (Amplified) are taken from The Amplified Bible. ©1965 by Zondervan Publishing House. Used by permission. All rights reserved.

ISBN-13: 978-1514241219

Jan Grace

Thanks...

To my wife, Phyllis. You have a way of making me look better than I really am. I sure am glad you're my wife.

Special thanks to Brian Davies, probably the strongest man I've ever met. He graciously allowed me to interrupt his workout, so I could take a picture of his muscular arm as he put it through the paces.

And of course, thanks to my Lord and Savior Jesus Christ. You've redeemed my life from destruction, and crowned me with Your tender mercies and grace.

Jan Grace

Table of Contents

INTRODUCTION	9
THE SIN ISSUE	13
ARM YOURSELVES	19
SUBMIT TO THE WORD	25
IN THE VOLUME OF THE BOOK	33
THE ROLE OF THE MIND	41
ABLE TO HEAR	47
HOW TO - AS TAUGHT BY THE TEACHER	55
FIVE THINGS	71
THE STORMY TEST	81
ADDITIONAL TRAINING AND TESTS	91
PREPARE THE WAY OF THE LORD	105
FINISHING WELL	111

Introduction

There's much talk these days about weapons, arms, guns, the Second Amendment, who should or shouldn't carry, and the rationing of ammunition. "We need to be able to protect our property and our family", people say. "The country's Founding Fathers knew the value of bearing arms; and it's a right many have fought and died for", others cry.

I am all for upholding the constitution. I have no problem with law abiding citizens owning guns.

But unfortunately, not everyone who carries a gun has the right intentions. Not everyone is packing for defense.

The same thing is true in the spirit world. Whether we like it or not, the unseen world is full of schemers and manipulators, armed with the tricks of their trade. Their goal is to disrupt the work of God using whatever means they can.

How do they do it? Why does it seem so hard to resist their attacks? Is there anything we can do to overcome these spiritual felons? Is there a pattern to their behavior; a particular "modus operandi"?

These questions are addressed within the pages of this book. Understanding certain principles, as revealed throughout the scripture, will help you "grow in the grace (God's willingness to use His power and ability on our behalf) and knowledge of our Lord and Savior, Jesus Christ" (2 Peter 3:18).

All scripture is given by inspiration of God, and is profitable... that the man of God may be perfect, thoroughly furnished unto all good works. (2 Timothy 3:16-17)

Grace and peace be multiplied unto you through the knowledge of God, and of Jesus our Lord, according as his divine power hath given unto us all things that pertain unto life and godliness, through the knowledge of him that hath called us to glory and virtue: whereby are given unto us exceeding great and precious promises: that by these ye might be partakers of the divine nature, having escaped the corruption that is in the world through lust. (2 Peter 1:2-3)

He's given us all things that pertain to life and godliness...to enable us to escape the corruption that's in the world. We can bring glory to God in everything we think, say, and do.

It's time to rise up in the Name of Jesus and act like the people God created us to be. We are new creations in Christ. We are more than conquerors through Him Who loved us. We are a chosen generation, a royal priesthood, and a holy nation. God's purchased possession. We can, by the power of the indwelling Spirit, have the mind of Christ and participate with God in bringing His Kingdom's authority and rule into this world. "Thy Kingdom come, Thy will be done in earth as it is in Heaven."

If you will apply the principles outlined herein, you will find yourself armed and ready for whatever comes your way; thoroughly prepared for every good work, AND to do the will of God. His glory is revealed as His will is accomplished in the earth; in our lives.

Armed for victory, armed with the mind of Christ, armed for glory.

God's glory revealed in and through us.

Jan Grace

THE SIN ISSUE

People look at me like I've lost it when I say, "We don't have to sin!" And I understand why. It's such a part of our mentality, our mindset, that we find the idea impossible to envision. "We can be sinless? Yeah, right. And I have a bridge I'd like to sell you."

But it's true. Jesus didn't just die and rise, leaving an empty tomb, so we could be forgiven and taken to Heaven when our life on this planet is finished. He came to address the sin issue.

It was sin, Adam's refusal to obey God, his rebellion against the known will of God, that transformed God's magnificent creation into a chaotic war zone. Everything changed the moment Adam ate from the Tree of the Knowledge of Good and Evil. Man's image was altered. Where light, revelation, complete peace and wholeness once reigned, it was overcome by darkness, ignorance, and brokenness.

But thanks be to God. He sent His Son Jesus, the last Adam, to seek and save that which was lost. He came to destroy the works of the devil. He came to annihilate the age old sin nature of mankind. And He did, through the death, burial, and resurrection of Jesus Christ.

For sin shall not have dominion over you: for ye are not under the law, but under grace. (Romans 6:14)

"Sin shall not have dominion over you...", or "Sin shall not rule you. It shall not dominate you. It is no longer the boss, the lord of your life. Neither the world, the flesh, nor the devil can make you disobey God." Sin should not ride roughshod over you.

Why? "Because you are not under the law, but under grace."

We used to have no defense; sooner or later we were bound to give in to the inward and outward desires of our flesh and mind. But as new creations in Christ, all that has changed. Sin isn't on top of us; God's grace is.

And His grace gives us all the help we need. The law could only point out God's holiness and our shortcomings. His righteousness and our unrighteousness. But His grace brings us the help we need, when we need it, to think, say, and do the right thing.

Notice the theme of the following scriptures:

Let the wicked forsake his way, and the unrighteous man his thoughts: and let him return unto the LORD, and he will have mercy upon him; and to our God, for he will abundantly pardon. For my thoughts are not your thoughts, neither are your ways my ways, saith the LORD. For as the heavens are higher than the earth, so are my ways higher than your ways, and my thoughts than your thoughts. (Isaiah 55:7-9)

We are to exchange our thoughts for God's thoughts; our ways for His. Leaving our old way of doing things, and allowing the grace of God to reveal a new, powerful and clean way of living.

Let us therefore come boldly unto the throne of grace, that we may obtain mercy, and find grace to help in time of need. (Hebrews 4:16)

God's invitation to His throne of mercy AND grace; grace to HELP. When is grace available? Whenever it is needed.

When might we need it? When we're faced with a challenge, a decision. Like Adam in the Garden of Eden. Like Jesus in the Garden of Gethsemane. Whenever or wherever, His grace is sufficient. His grace is more than enough to meet the challenge.

And God is able to make all grace abound toward you; that ye, always having all sufficiency in all things, may abound to every good work: (2 Corinthians 9:8)

And he said unto me, My grace is sufficient for thee: for my strength is made perfect in weakness. Most gladly therefore will I rather glory in my infirmities, that the power of Christ may rest upon me. Therefore I take pleasure in infirmities, in reproaches, in necessities, in persecutions, in distresses for Christ's sake: for when I am weak, then am I strong. (2 Corinthians 12:9-10)

Before we go any further, let me remind you that sin is not necessarily a deed done by someone who is perverted or deranged. It could be something socially acceptable; like worry, for instance. In many cases it's the motive behind the action. The motive could be fear, selfishness, greed, lust, or whatever. And remember, "...whatever is not of faith is sin" (Romans 14:23).

Father God has done His part in addressing the sin issue. First of all, to undo the damage caused when Adam yielded to the old serpent, God needed someone who could identify with Adam's race (a human being) as well as deity. Someone who would act as a mediator, a go between; a representative for God and man. Jesus, conceived by the Spirit, born of a virgin, was God's answer. And ours.

For there is one God, and one mediator between God and men, the man Christ Jesus (1 Timothy 2:5).

Christ Jesus lived His spotless, sinless life as Adam could

have done had he relied upon the Father's word. And when Jesus was nailed to the cross, He carried the punishment due all mankind, from Adam to the very last person who'll ever be born.

Jesus, with God's help, tasted death for every human being. The Sinless took the place of the sinner. The obedient one covered for the rebel. And God shouted, "AMEN!" to the world when He raised Jesus from the dead. Death couldn't hold the Obedient One.

The devil couldn't master Jesus in death, because he was not able to master Him in life. And he can't master you in death if he's lost his hold on your life.

The sin issue was dealt a death blow. Through faith in Christ, sons and daughters of God have been giving the devil nightmares for the past 2,000 years. Every man, woman, and child born of God through faith in Jesus Christ has the privilege and responsibility to follow, as disciples of Jesus, His example and testimony of victory over sin. To do God's will, regardless. To overcome the world, the flesh, and the devil.

But as many as received him, to them gave he power to become the sons of God, even to them that believe on his name: (John 1:12)

For if by one man's offence death reigned by one; much more they which receive abundance of grace and of the gift of righteousness shall reign in life by one, Jesus

Christ. (Romans 5:17)

This is a far cry from what many well meaning Christians would have us believe.

I'm not saying it's an easy thing; to go through life without sinning. Nor am I saying that I've attained the high and holy mark of sinlessness. But God's word is clear. It's principles are applicable to the world we live in. And God's grace hasn't changed.

The sin issue has been addressed, and Jesus is our way out! So get ready to read, pray, and meditate. Change is on the way, along with victory and joy.

ARM YOURSELVES

Forasmuch then as Christ hath suffered for us in the flesh, arm yourselves likewise with the same mind: for he that hath suffered in the flesh hath ceased from sin; that he no longer should live the rest of his time in the flesh to the lusts of men, but to the will of God. (1 Peter 4:1-2)

When did Christ suffer for us in the flesh? At Pilate's Judgment Hall? Yes. On the cross? Yes. But there were many other times as well.

He suffered every time someone mocked and ridiculed Him. He suffered in the Garden, pleading with His Father for another way to bring salvation to all mankind. He suffered in the wilderness, being tempted by the devil. He suffered when He heard the news of His cousin's murder; and although He wanted to get away for a time and be alone, He yielded to His Father's will and ministered to the multitudes who had tracked Him down.

He suffered when He heard Lazarus was dead. He suffered when His close friends wouldn't believe. He suffered as He looked over Jerusalem, knowing that many would reject the Peace Offering God had extended to them.

He suffered in the flesh each time He was tempted. It was either that, or give in to the flesh. But suffering in the flesh made it possible for Him to do the will of God.

And so it is with you and I.

Does it bother you to think that Jesus was tempted? Well, He was.

For we have not an high priest which cannot be touched with the feeling of our infirmities; but was in all points tempted like as we are, yet without sin. (Hebrews 4:15)

He was tempted, but didn't for a moment yield or give in. Though His flesh wanted to go one way, He wouldn't allow it. He suffered by not allowing His flesh to dominate. Sin did not have dominion over Him!

Peter wrote, "...arm yourselves likewise with the same mind...". The same mind of Christ. The word "arm" means to prepare your mind as a weapon for righteousness. Use your mind to combat the desires of the flesh, and the temptations which may come at you from all sides. By arming yourselves, you will no longer live giving in to sin, but will instead bring glory to God by doing His will.

Notice how Jesus armed Himself with His Father's mind. In Matthew chapter three, as Jesus was baptized by John, the voice of the Father was heard saying, "This is My beloved Son, in whom I am well pleased." That's all Jesus needed to hear to prepare Himself for what was to come.

Then Jesus was led up by the Spirit into the wilderness to be tempted by the devil. And when He had fasted forty days and forty nights, afterward He was hungry. Now when the tempter came to Him, he said, "If You are the Son of God, command that these stones become bread." But He answered and said, "It is written, 'Man shall not live by bread alone, but by every word that proceeds from the mouth of God'" (Matthew 4:1-4 NKJV).

The devil challenged the Father's word. "If you be...". It's the way he operates. It's how he worked in the Garden of Eden, and it's how he works with you and I. It's why we must arm ourselves with the mind of Christ.

Jesus told the devil, "I don't live by your instructions or promises. I don't live by the dictates of my flesh. I live by what proceeds from My Father's mouth. He's already told Me I'm His Son and that's good enough for Me. I'm hungry, but not hungry enough to quit trusting My Father's word."

Here's a well known passage from Proverbs.

Trust in the LORD with all thine heart; and lean not unto thine own understanding. In all thy ways acknowledge him, and he shall direct thy paths. Be not wise in thine own eyes: fear the LORD, and depart from evil. (Proverbs 3:5-7)

Trust and lean not...be not wise in your own eyes (or in your own estimation). One cannot fear the Lord and ignore what He says. We may not understand everything about a certain temptation, struggle, or challenge. That's where the "suffering in the flesh" comes into play. But the more we do what He says, the more we'll depart from evil.

Once again, evil is not just some deep, dark perversion. Evil isn't limited to such atrocities as murder, rape, or incest. While those things are horrendous, evil could also be something as simple as not giving someone ten dollars. What?!? Yes. If the word proceeding from the mouth of God (or, God's will) spoke to your heart and instructed you to give so and so a ten dollar bill, and you reasoned in your heart that you couldn't afford it or they didn't deserve it, you did evil.

I didn't say it was as if you murdered someone.

I just said you did evil. And it's something we're all capable of, unless we arm ourselves with the same mind as Christ.

There are some who, when they hear, "God wants you free of sin", seem to gain much relief by reminding everyone, "All have sinned and come short of the Glory of God."

Of course it's true. All have sinned.

But God doesn't intend for us to stay there - apart from the Glory.

In fact, when God's will is done, His Glory is revealed. When we obey Him, He's glorified in and through us. And the more we walk in obedience to His word, His will, the more He's glorified.

SUBMIT TO THE WORD

Forasmuch then as Christ hath suffered for us in the flesh, arm yourselves likewise with the same mind: for he that hath suffered in the flesh hath ceased from sin; that he no longer should live the rest of his time in the flesh to the lusts of men, but to the will of God. (1 Peter 4:1-2)

Before we discuss the mind's role in overcoming temptation, or in fulfilling God's will for our lives, we must understand the value of God's word. If we are going to DO God's will, we must KNOW His will. His word is His will. If we are to be able to discern His inward voice, we must know God's word. If we are ever going to have faith, mountain-moving, devil-chasing, world-changing faith, we MUST know God's word.

In a sense, God's word must be our Master.

It would be good for you to take a moment, break away from this book, pick up your bible and read the book of First Peter. I will refer to some of these scriptures throughout this chapter.

Everything seen and unseen was created by the word of God. "In the beginning was the Word...and the Word was God" (John 1:1). God spoke, releasing His will through His carefully formed words, and "it was so."

Everything is upheld by the power of His word.

"...[U]pholding all things by the power of His word..." (Hebrews 1:3).

Jesus said, "Heaven and earth will pass away, but My words will by no means pass away." (Matthew 24:35 NKJV)

It's the Word (the incorruptible seed) that is instrumental in helping each child of God grow into a disciplined son or daughter of the Most High God:

Being born again, not of corruptible seed, but of incorruptible, by the word of God, which liveth and abideth for ever. For all flesh is as grass, and all the glory of man as the flower of grass. The grass withereth, and the flower thereof falleth away: but the word of the Lord endureth for ever. And this is the word which by the gospel is preached unto you. Wherefore laying aside all malice, and all guile, and hypocrisies, and envies, and all evil speakings, as newborn babes, desire the sincere milk of the word, that ye may grow thereby: if so be ye have tasted that the Lord is gracious. (1 Peter 1:23-2:3)

Peter writes at least three chapters (chapters 2-4), describing what it means to be in submission to God's word. It may not appear as though he's talking about submitting to the Word, but that's exactly what he means.

The word of God should be the only master we submit to. It MUST be, for it is the very thing that causes people to be born again; born of God.

I'll show you what I mean.

To tell God and everyone else that God is your master, and yet not do what He said, is hypocritical at best; and it could be just plain out and out lying. Jesus said, "Why do you call Me, Lord, Lord, and not do the things that I say?" (Luke 6:46). In other words, "Why do you call Me your Supreme Commander and not take My words seriously?" Good question for us all, don't you think?

The words, "submit", "submission", and "subjection", simply mean "under obedience", or "subordinate oneself". To (voluntarily) place oneself under the authority of another.

By the way, one way or another, everyone will eventually be in subjection to the Word and to Jesus Christ.

Faith in Jesus should automatically mean submission to His word. For instance:

Therefore, to you who believe, He is precious; but to those who are disobedient, "The stone which the builders rejected has become the chief cornerstone," and, "A stone of stumbling and a rock of offense." They stumble, being disobedient to the word, to which they also were appointed. (1 Peter 2:7-8 NKJV)

"Believe" is a word we probably all understand. At least we think we do. But what about the word "disobedient"? It is the antithesis of the word "believe". Did you catch that? Believing, according to the word of God, includes obedience; while "disobedience" means "not believing."

I'll explain. The Greek word for believe is "pisteuo", meaning "believe". The Greek word for "disobedient" (as used above in verse 7) is "apisteo", meaning "unbelieving". This principle is shown throughout the word of God. To believe God is to obey God; otherwise, one must question if faith is truly present.

If a person truly believes, commitment is not a problem. If commitment isn't a problem, then obedience will happen. Obedience to the Word is another way of saying "submitting to the Word"; or allowing the word of God to be the Master of our life.

Submission to the Word is described in a number of different ways throughout Peter's first epistle. After he writes about being born again of the incorruptible seed, the word of God, he continues by telling the readers to "desire the pure milk of the Word, so you may grow...".

Note how he speaks of submission to Christ and His word:

1. 1 Peter 2:4 - Coming to Him...
2. Verse 5 - Living stones (just like Christ, the chief cornerstone) used by God to build as He sees fit
3. Verses 6-8 - Believing contrasted with disobedience - believing the Word as opposed to stumbling (disobeying, turning from, apostatizing)
4. Verse 11,12 - Abstain (distance yourself) from... to a place where your conduct is honorable - Christlike
5. Verses 13-15 - Submission to man's laws for the Lord's sake...for it's the will of God, that by doing good... Notice - the result of obeying God's word, His will, is good
6. Verses 18-23 - A word to servants (all of us) - be UNDER OBEDIENCE to your masters...

Let's look at verse 18 a bit differently - "Servants of Christ, be submissive to your master, the word of God...not only to the good, easygoing, promises of blessing and abundance, but also to the words that are hard to understand, that don't make sense, and are hard on the flesh. The ones like, 'Take up your cross and follow Me.'"

Submission. And like I mentioned before, submission ultimately begins by submitting to God and His word.

"Wives...be submissive to your own husbands" (3:1,5). At first glance the command seems rather oppressive for the woman, but not if you understand the full extent of her submission. She is to submit to the Word FIRST.

AFTERWARD, "...when they observe your chaste conduct..." (v. 2). Chaste, clean, pure, even disciplined conduct; the result of submitting FIRST to God's word, His authority. That is how the husband is able to recognize a power greater than himself, and thus submit to the Lordship of Jesus.

"Husbands, LIKEWISE..." (v. 7). Submit to the Word, and dwelling with your wife won't be near the problem it would otherwise be.

"Finally, all of you be of one mind..." (v. 8). Another way of saying it is, "Submitting to one another in the fear of God" (Ephesians 5:21).

Notice these words and phrases scattered throughout the remainder of First Peter:

"Followers of what is good" - 3:13
"Sanctify the Lord God (set apart)..." - v.15
"Suffer for doing good..." - v.17
"Having been made subject to Him" - v.22
"But for the will of God" - 4:2
"Partake in Christ's sufferings" - v.13
"But let none of you suffer as a murderer..." - v.15
"Yet if anyone suffers as a Christian, let him not be

ashamed" - v.16
"Let those who suffer according to the will of God..." - v.19

Suffering, as a result of submission to the Word and will of God, is something that really excites God. Not the act of suffering, or pain inflicted; but the submission to His will regardless of what may happen.

It's what Jesus did. He suffered in the flesh because He was determined to do God's will.

THAT is the mind we are to arm ourselves with. Submission to God's word.

"Submit to your elders" - 5:5
"Yes, all of you be submissive to one another, and clothed with humility" - v.5
"Humble yourselves under the mighty hand of God" - v.6
"Be sober, be vigilant..." - v.8

Everything points to submitting to God and His word. Even resisting the devil, steadfast in the faith, requires us to FIRST humble ourselves before God.

I have NO power over the devil, if God has no power over me. To be over, one must FIRST be under. Authority and power from God are only given to those who will humble themselves UNDER His mighty hand.

Submit to the Word. Let God's word be your master. Let it rule your life.

Jan Grace

IN THE VOLUME OF THE BOOK

For the law, having a shadow of the good things to come, and not the very image of the things, can never with these same sacrifices, which they offer continually year by year, make those who approach perfect. For then would they not have ceased to be offered? For the worshipers, once purified, would have had no more consciousness of sins. But in those sacrifices there is a reminder of sins every year. For it is not possible that the blood of bulls and goats could take away sins.

Therefore, when He came into the world, He said: "Sacrifice and offering You did not desire, but a body You have prepared for Me. In burnt offerings and sacrifices for sin You had no pleasure. Then I said, 'Behold, I have come — in the volume of the book it is written of Me — to do Your will, O God.'"

Previously saying, "Sacrifice and offering, burnt

offerings, and offerings for sin You did not desire, nor had pleasure in them" (which are offered according to the law), then He said, "Behold, I have come to do Your will, O God." He takes away the first that He may establish the second. By that will we have been sanctified through the offering of the body of Jesus Christ once for all. (Hebrews 10:1-10 NKJV)

One of the tools Jesus used to guard His heart, protect His mission, and please His Father is the "Volume of the Book." Tools may not be the best word; disciplines is probably better.

There's a passage in Luke's gospel that demonstrates this.

And there was delivered unto him the book of the prophet Esaias. And when he had opened the book, he found the place where it was written; (Luke 4:17)

Reading from Isaiah 61, He says, "The Spirit of the Lord is upon Me, and He has anointed Me to preach... heal... deliver... and declare the Lord's favor..."

Notice, He found where it was written. He knew the Volume of the Book was His purpose, His life. After all, He was the Word made flesh.

Acts 10:38 reads, "How God anointed Jesus of Nazareth with the Holy Ghost and with power; Who went about doing good and healing all that were oppressed of the devil; for God was with Him."

He armed Himself with the "Body" His Father had prepared for Him; found in the Volume of the Book.

His Father referred to Him as the Serpent Smasher, Genesis 3:15. Jesus was armed to do that very thing. He came to DESTROY the works of the devil.

And then shall that Wicked be revealed, whom the Lord shall consume with the spirit of his mouth, and shall destroy with the brightness of his coming: (2 Thessalonians 2:8)

Forasmuch then as the children are partakers of flesh and blood, he also himself likewise took part of the same; that through death he might destroy him that had the power of death, that is, the devil; (Hebrews 2:14)

He that committeth sin is of the devil; for the devil sinneth from the beginning. For this purpose the Son of God was manifested, that he might destroy the works of the devil. (1 John 3:8)

He was Abraham's Ram, caught in the thicket; God Almighty's provision for all mankind. He was the Tree Moses saw in Exodus 15, which changed the waters from bitter to sweet. He was the Serpent on the pole in Numbers 21, and whoever believed was saved and healed.

Not sure about the Serpent on the pole? Read John 3:14 and 2 Corinthians 5:21.

He was the Light to the nations, the Balm of Gilead, the Suffering Servant, and the Glorious King. He walked the shores of Galilee in the same manner He carried the cross to Calvary - with faith and purpose.

He was armed.

"Behold, I have come - in the Volume of the Book it is written of Me - to do Your will, O God."

In the Volume of the Book, all 66 books of the Bible, you'll find not only Jesus' earthly purpose in life; you'll also find YOURS.

In the Volume of the Book, it is written of YOU. Your development, your purpose, your manner of living, and your destiny as a son or daughter of Almighty God.

Regardless of who you are, or what your background is; in the Volume of the Book it is written of YOU. And in the Volume of the Book is where you'll find your ammunition for any attack.

I'll show you what I mean.

First of all, there's this thing called predestination. No, not as if you have no choice. But predestination as far as what God has planned, ordained, PREDESTINED for all who are in Christ Jesus.

For whom he did foreknow, he also did predestinate to

be conformed to the image of his Son, that he might be the firstborn among many brethren. (Romans 8:29)

God the Father has established what each of His sons and daughters will look like, act like, BE like when He's completed His work in us; conformed (formed) into the image of His Son. Like Adam was originally, created in the image of God, so we are predestined to be conformed into the image of the Last Adam; Jesus, the Christ.

So, based on the Father's intentions, as revealed in His word, we'll look throughout the Volume of the Book and see what's written about us. Just as Jesus was armed with "You ARE My beloved Son, in whom I AM WELL PLEASED", so our spirit needs to be saturated with His word about us.

Note: as you study this chapter, please don't limit your research to the scriptures listed in this book. I am not even attempting to include all that God has ordained for you and I. This chapter is meant to be a catalyst; helping you know what God has made possible for you, so you will dig into His word for yourself.

Glorious things are spoken of thee, O city of God. Selah. (Psalms 87:3)

And glorious things are spoken of THEE, O child of God! You'll find them in the Volume of the Book.

1. Blessed with believing Abraham - Galatians 3:9-29

This includes redemption from the curse of the law (v.13) and the promise of the Spirit (v.14). God told Abraham, "I am your Shield, your exceedingly great reward." He made a covenant with Abraham (though, according to Galatians 3, He was also making it with Abraham's SEED, Jesus).

God is OUR Shield, OUR exceedingly great reward, through our union with Christ, Abraham's seed. He's our Protector, Provider; our all in all.

Here are some other things to contemplate:

2. The Glory of God is revealed in us - Romans 8:18; Colossians 1:27
3. We belong to God, so we can be led by the Spirit of God - Romans 8:5-14
4. We're never separated from the Love of God - Romans 8:39
5. We are free from the Law of sin and death - Romans 8:1,2
6. We can know the things of God - 1 Corinthians 2:10-12
7. We are washed, sanctified, and justified in the Name of the Lord - 1 Corinthians 6:9-11
8. We're comforted in all our tribulations - 2 Corinthians 1:3,4
9. The God Who said, "Light BE", has shown His light in our hearts - 2 Corinthians 4:6
10. We're a new creation, His ambassador - 2 Corinthians 5:17-21
11. We are blessed with every spiritual blessing in Christ - Ephesians 1:3

12. We are raised to sit with Christ in heavenly places - Ephesians 1:20
13. We are His workmanship - Ephesians 2:10
14. We are delivered from Satan's authority - Colossians 1:13
15. We are dead, and our life is hidden with Christ - Colossians 3:3
16. We are the ELECT (favored, favorite) of God - Colossians 3:12
17. We are sons of light, and sons of the day - 1 Thessalonians 5:5
18. We ALWAYS have an open door to Father - Hebrews 4:16; 1 John 2:1
19. His divine power has given us all things... - 2 Peter 1:2-4
20. We are world overcomers - 1 John 5:1-5

Glorious things are spoken of you, Child of God. Find them in the Volume of the Book. Find out how to walk and talk as one of God's children. Learn what to think, what to believe.

Arm yourselves with God's truth about the world, the flesh, the devil, AND His truth regarding YOU!

Remember, Paul wrote:

There hath no temptation taken you but such as is common to man: but God is faithful, who will not suffer you to be tempted above that ye are able; but will with the temptation also make a way to escape, that ye may be able to bear it. (1 Corinthians 10:13)

A great and effective way to deal with temptation, to either bear it or escape from it, is to do what Jesus did. For how did Jesus know His purpose in life, but by spending time in the Word? Luke wrote, "[Jesus] increased in wisdom and stature, and in favor with God and man." Jesus knew that in the Volume of the Book it was written of Him. You and I need to know it as well.

One more thing before we dive into the Role of the Mind. If you and I will walk with God, we will ALWAYS be prepared for two things:

1. ANY temptation. It was Father who gave Jesus the answer to the devil's enticements, before the trip to the desert.

2. EVERY good work. "...That the man (or woman) of God may be mature, and thoroughly equipped for EVERY GOOD WORK." (2 Timothy 3:17)

In the Volume of the Book it is written about YOU. Find out what it says, and act accordingly.

THE ROLE OF THE MIND

Forasmuch then as Christ hath suffered for us in the flesh, arm yourselves likewise with the same mind... (1 Peter 4:1)

What's so important about the mind? After all, the scriptures teach it's with the heart, not the mind, that man believes.

For with the heart one believes and is justified, and with the mouth one confesses and is saved. (Romans 10:10 ESV)

Yes, it's the heart that believes. It's the heart that stores up the treasures of God. It's the heart that becomes ignited with the presence of God.

But the mind is also important.

It's the mind that instructs your mouth to speak the praises of God. It's the mind that gives direction to your body, cooperating with your heart to accomplish the will of God. It is the mind that determines to follow the leading of your heart, or the temptations of your flesh.

And be not conformed to this world: but be ye transformed by the renewing of your mind, that ye may prove what is that good, and acceptable, and perfect, will of God. (Romans 12:2)

A person is transformed, not only by believing with the heart, but by renewing their mind with the word of God.

Phillips translation of Romans 12:2 reads like this:

Don't let the world around you squeeze you into its own mold, but let God remold your minds from within, so that you may prove in practice that the plan of God for you is good, meets all his demands and moves toward the goal of true maturity.

For instance, the people from Berea (Acts 17:11) received the Word with all readiness and eagerness of mind; ready to put it to good use.

Paul wrote in Romans 8:6, "For to be carnally minded is death; but to be spiritually minded is life and peace." The emphasis is not only on what a person believes. The belief itself will not guarantee anyone a victorious life in Christ. James tells us to be doers of the Word (James 1:22).

Though the scripture says, "This is the victory that has overcome the world, even our faith" (1 John 5:4), understand it's impossible to have world-overcoming faith without the mind of Christ.

Let this mind be in you, which was also in Christ Jesus: (Philippians 2:5)

If you will continue reading in Philippians, you'll notice that Christ's mind helped Him lay down His reputation, pick up the form of a servant, and humble Himself to a life of complete obedience; even laying His life down for you and I.

That's the mind we are to arm ourselves with. A mind so connected to the word and will of God that nothing is allowed to move us from side to side.

Philippians, chapter four, instructs us to:

[B]e careful (anxious) for nothing; but in everything by prayer and supplication with thanksgiving let your requests be made known unto God. And the peace of God, which passeth all understanding, shall keep your hearts and minds through Christ Jesus (Philippians 4:6-7).

Imagine the ramifications. Our heart AND mind calm, cool, and collected.

Then, to kind of top it all off, Paul continues:

Finally, brethren, whatsoever things are true, whatsoever things are honest, whatsoever things are just, whatsoever things are pure, whatsoever things are lovely, whatsoever things are of good report; if there be any virtue, and if there be any praise, think on these things. (Philippians 4:8)

Think on these things. THINK. Use your mind.

The writer of the book of Hebrews reminds us of the troubled Israelites during the Exodus. Israel had been instructed by God, through Moses, to spy out the Land of Promise and bring back the report (Numbers 13,14).

Now, mind you, the reconnaissance team had heard Moses speak of the great land God was bringing them into. They'd heard Moses preach, "God is bringing you out, to bring you in." They had witnessed all the miracles of protection and provision. Now they were on their way to see firsthand just what a glorious land it was.

But when, after forty days, they returned with a "but" report, something evil took over. You're not sure what a "but" report is? "God said this, BUT..." That's a "but" report.

The report was evil.

By the way, if you stop and think about it for a moment, you'll recognize the similarity between an evil report and the devil's words to Eve. "God said it, BUT..."

An innocent sounding statement? Yes. However, it was AN EVIL word that caused people to distrust and disobey God.

Even those men that did bring up the evil report upon the land, died by the plague before the LORD. (Numbers 14:37)

Evil, not because they wanted to murder someone, but because it kept them from doing the will of God.

Evil because they didn't mix faith with God's word.

For unto us was the gospel preached, as well as unto them: but the word preached did not profit them, not being mixed with faith in them that heard it. (Hebrews 4:2)

The Israelites had heard the good news of the Promised Land, but didn't mix faith with that word. Where was the disconnect? In their minds.

We must use our mind when it's time to mix faith with God's word. For faith to have full expression in our lives, and for the impossible to become possible, we must arm ourselves with the mind of Christ. If we are to live a life that pleases God in all things, a renewed, armed mind is essential.

ABLE TO HEAR

As a teenager, I wasn't the world's best student. Not in the least. In fact, it was easy for me to drift in and out of class without leaving the room. I could sit and daydream for hours, fantasizing about all the things I'd rather be doing.

Present, yet absent.

If I was seated next to a window, I might as well have played hooky that day. I could hear the noise of someone talking, but my mind was miles away.

Even today, I can act in somewhat the same manner. In fact, when my wife and I go out to eat, and it's just the two of us, she will have me sit facing a wall or if possible, my back to all TV's. She likes to have my undivided attention.

Most of the time her strategy works.

I'm sure I'm not the only person to act in such a way. It's a fairly common trait. People are easily distracted. Maybe even more so with all the electronic gadgets we carry around. Much of the time it may not be a big deal, that we are sidetracked so easily. But when a loved one wants to speak to us, we need to be able to hear what they're trying to communicate. It could even be a matter of life and death!

That's why Jesus prefaced many of His teachings with the phrase, "He who has ears, let him hear."

In Mark chapter four, as Jesus taught on the Kingdom of God and the word of God, He emphasized the importance of hearing. "Listen", "Behold", "He who has ears", "Take heed", "As they were able to hear", "He explained…" As a teacher, Jesus was trying to get His class to listen and learn the lessons.

And with many such parables He spoke the word to them as they were able to hear it. (Mark 4:33 NKJV)

I find the phrase, "as they were able to hear it", quite interesting. The word translated, "able", is from a Greek word "dunamai", a form of the Greek word "dunamis", from which we get our English word dynamite. It actually means, "to be able, or possible". But I see something else about that word. Just like the resurrected Jesus told the disciples, "You shall receive power (dunamis) when the Holy Spirit has come upon you…" (Acts 1:8), I recognize the need for the Holy Spirit to help us hear the word He's wanting to teach us.

But, like I said, it's so easy to be distracted.

Keeping ourselves in a ready position to hear the Teacher every time He attempts to teach us can be a real chore. Remember in school when the teachers would tell us to sit up straight, hands on the table, feet on the floor, and eyes straight ahead? They were teaching us the proper posture so we'd get the most out of the lessons.

The Lord does the same thing.

My son, attend to my words; incline thine ear unto my sayings. Let them not depart from thine eyes; keep them in the midst of thine heart. (Proverbs 4:20-21)

Pay attention, lean in to what He is saying, and never look away. Good advice, eh?

In Ezekiel, chapter 37, the Lord spoke to Ezekiel and showed him a valley of dry bones.

Again he said unto me, "Prophesy upon these bones, and say unto them, O ye dry bones, hear the word of the Lord." (Ezekiel 37:4)

The Lord told Ezekiel to prophesy, or speak by divine inspiration and revelation. He was to tell the nation of Israel exactly and only what the Lord told him to say.

The first thing Ezekiel told them was, "Hear the word of the Lord." An important thing to remember, God was in the process of restoring the nation of Israel back into fellowship with Him, and a place of greatness in the world. So, "Hear the word of the Lord" was key.

And it is key for us. If we are going to be able to stand against every scheme of the enemy, armed with the mind of Christ, we MUST hear the word of the Lord. Remember Matthew 4:4; man lives by what proceeds from the mouth of the Lord.

The word "hear", used in Ezekiel 37 and a number of other places throughout the Old Testament, is the Hebrew word "shama", which means "to hear intelligently, with the purpose of learning what to do so you can obey it." Or, in other words, "listen carefully, so you can obey intentionally." Hearing and obeying. Not one without the other. So, in essence Ezekiel was saying, "Hear and obey what God is telling you this day."

The word "shama" is also used in Deuteronomy when the Lord says, "Hear O Israel, the Lord is One."

Another example, and very fitting for us in this day and age, is found in Judges, chapter one.

Now after the death of Joshua it came to pass, that the children of Israel asked the Lord, saying, "Who shall go up for us against the Canaanites first, to fight against them?" And the Lord said, "Judah shall go up: behold, I have delivered the land into his hand." And Judah said unto Simeon his brother, "Come up with me into my lot, that we may fight against the Canaanites; and I likewise will go with thee into thy lot." So Simeon went with him. And Judah went up; and the Lord delivered the Canaanites and the Perizzites into their hand: and they slew of them in Bezek ten thousand men. (Judges 1:1-4)

Two of the twelve tribes of Israel are mentioned in this passage; Judah and Simeon. Each of the names had a specific meaning. Judah meant "praise" and Simeon meant "hearing". Simeon is the same Hebrew word, "shama", which we looked at earlier.

Notice the setting. After Joshua passed away, there was still land to conquer and occupy. Judah was instructed to lead out and take on the Canaanites. Judah sized up the enemy and asked their brothers for help, knowing they would in turn help them.

At times God's people think they can simply sing their way to victory. The enemy comes at them, so they put on their favorite praise and worship CD, and sing their hearts out.

Unfortunately, victory isn't always that simple.

Sometimes there is a word we must hear and obey WHILE worshiping the Lord. One word comes to mind as I write: "Trust".

Praise and worship isn't the same as praise and worry.

I've been caught by the Holy Spirit "praising" and worrying at the same time. Singing His praises while processing my own ideas and notions in my mind.

Have YOU been guilty of "hearing" God's word through these filters?

1. Preconceived ideas and notions - absolutely convinced we know everything there is to know about a particular subject. When we listen to a sermon, we listen through the filter of our own experience and knowledge. When we read, the words are kept within the framework of our past learning; we are unable to conceive in our mind there may be something we're missing and need to learn.

2. No intention of obeying - excited to read and hear the word of the Lord, but not inclined to let anyone tell us what to do. We'll figure it out for ourselves, and ONLY then will we jump into the thing called obedience.

The Teacher is trying to train us to live righteously and soberly in this mean, nasty, ugly world. If we're going to be trained, we MUST learn to hear AND obey. We MUST be doers of the Word, not just hearers only (James 1).

Cooperating with the Lord, and His Spirit of Truth, will help us grow in grace and the knowledge of His will. We can get to the place where even our senses (our flesh) are capable of discerning what's good and what's evil; what's of God and what isn't.

But strong meat belongeth to them that are of full age, even those who by reason of use have their senses exercised to discern both good and evil. (Hebrews 5:14)

"By reason of use...". Make certain you are able to hear, and ready to obey what you hear. Use what the Teacher tells you.

And you'll find yourself "armed with the mind of Christ".

Now, on to the "How To" portion of this book.

How To - As Taught By The Teacher

There's a parable Jesus taught, in Mark, chapter four, that I like to refer to as the Parable of Parables. Jesus said it this way:

If you can't understand the meaning of this parable, how will you understand all the other parables? (Mark 4:13 NLT)

In other words, the key to the other parables Jesus taught is the one found in Mark 4:3-9, and explained in Mark 4:14-20. It's the parable of the sower sowing the Word. Or if you will, the farmer planting the seed.

Here's the parable, and Jesus' explanation.

Once again Jesus began teaching by the lake shore. A very large crowd soon gathered around him, so he got into a boat. Then he sat in the boat while all the people remained on the shore. He taught them by telling many stories in the form of parables, such as this one:

"Listen! A farmer went out to plant some seed. As he scattered it across his field, some of the seed fell on a footpath, and the birds came and ate it. Other seed fell on shallow soil with underlying rock. The seed sprouted quickly because the soil was shallow. But the plant soon wilted under the hot sun, and since it didn't have deep roots, it died. Other seed fell among thorns that grew up and choked out the tender plants so they produced no grain. Still other seeds fell on fertile soil, and they sprouted, grew, and produced a crop that was thirty, sixty, and even a hundred times as much as had been planted!" Then he said, "Anyone with ears to hear should listen and understand."

Later, when Jesus was alone with the twelve disciples and with the others who were gathered around, they asked him what the parables meant.

He replied, "You are permitted to understand the secret of the Kingdom of God. But I use parables for everything I say to outsiders, so that the Scriptures might be fulfilled:

'When they see what I do, they will learn nothing. When they hear what I say, they will not understand. Otherwise, they will turn to me and be forgiven.'"

Then Jesus said to them, "If you can't understand the

meaning of this parable, how will you understand all the other parables? The farmer plants seed by taking God's word to others. The seed that fell on the footpath represents those who hear the message, only to have Satan come at once and take it away. The seed on the rocky soil represents those who hear the message and immediately receive it with joy. But since they don't have deep roots, they don't last long. They fall away as soon as they have problems or are persecuted for believing God's word. The seed that fell among the thorns represents others who hear God's word, but all too quickly the message is crowded out by the worries of this life, the lure of wealth, and the desire for other things, so no fruit is produced. And the seed that fell on good soil represents those who hear and accept God's word and produce a harvest of thirty, sixty, or even a hundred times as much as had been planted!" (Mark 4:1-20 NLT)

Please don't get me wrong, but one doesn't have to be a brain surgeon to comprehend this.

Farmers understand this parable, even if they've never read or heard it. They know a seed has to be planted, and the soil should be prepared as well as possible. They may not be able to explain exactly how or why the seed grows like it does, but they know it does. So they do their part, and let the seed do what it does best.

Grow.

There are six things I'd like for you to observe, all of

which are contained in Mark 4:13-34. Six things that will help you be prepared for anything the enemy may throw at you. Six things which will help you arm yourself with the mind of Christ, and thus win over every temptation.

Here they are:

1. The Word makes all the difference between winning or losing, life or death, living in the Spirit or in the flesh.

But he (Jesus) answered and said, "It is written, Man shall not live by bread alone, but by every word that proceedeth out of the mouth of God." (Matthew 4:4)

Compare this with what Jesus taught about the sower and the Word. There was nothing wrong with the Word (the seed). It grew even in unfavorable conditions and environments. Though it couldn't sustain growth or bear fruit in those bad conditions, there was nothing wrong with the Word. But remove the Word, or the seed, and even with the best conditions and environment nothing will ever be produced. One must have the seed to produce fruit. One must have the Word of God in their life if they are to grow in the things of God.

Jesus told the devil, "Look. Just because my stomach is screaming at me, I don't have to listen or obey it. Yes, I'm hungry. I'm VERY hungry. But I'm not hungry enough to follow your suggestions or enticements. Instead, I'm going to get my fill by feasting on what my Father is telling me. You see, I trust in the Lord with all my heart, and I don't lean on my own understanding. In all my ways I acknowledge Him, and He directs my paths. I'm not wise in my own eyes. I fear the Lord, and in doing so, I stay away from evil" (Proverbs 3:5-7).

Jesus armed Himself with His Father's mind. He knew the importance of the Father's word, and the necessity of keeping it in the midst of His heart. It's what Adam should have done centuries before, but didn't.

The Psalmist wrote, "Thy word have I hid in my heart that I might not sin against Thee." He knew the importance of the Word.

2. You MUST receive AND hold on to the Word.

For this cause also thank we God without ceasing, because, when ye received the word of God which ye heard of us, ye received it not as the word of men, but as it is in truth, the word of God, which effectually worketh also in you that believe. (1 Thessalonians 2:13)

I'm not referring to some type of mental assent when I speak of receiving the word of God. Actively receiving the Word is like actively receiving a gift from a friend. In other words, you don't just point at the person bearing the gift, mumbling something about putting the gift on the sofa or someplace out of the way; like you're not interested and you couldn't care less.

The way you value a gift will play a key role in how well

you receive it, or welcome it into your life. And the way you receive it will determine to what degree you'll go in order to keep it; to guard it.

If the Word isn't important to you, you'll never arm yourself with the mind of Christ; i.e. His word. If it isn't valued, you'll never make the time to sow it into your life. Or you'll develop an attitude that's something like this: "If I hear the Word, no big deal. If I don't, again no big deal. I'm saved, so whatever."

Sorry, but that is completely contrary to what Jesus taught in His Parable of Parables.

Then he added, "Pay close attention to what you hear. The closer you listen, the more understanding you will be given—and you will receive even more. To those who listen to my teaching, more understanding will be given. But for those who are not listening, even what little understanding they have will be taken away from them." (Mark 4:24-25 NLT)

Luke's account of this same passage reads just a little differently:

...But for those who are not listening, even what they think they understand will be taken away from them. Luke 8:18b NLT

"Even what they THINK they understand...". Gone. No fruit. Nothing to live on or live by. Empty, holey pockets.

Nothing left to work with. All because the Word isn't valued as it should be.

Jesus said, "Heaven and earth will pass away, but not a single word that I've spoken will" (Matthew 24:35 paraphrased). If it's more valuable and powerful than heaven and earth, I believe it is something we should make certain we know how to receive AND keep.

Back to the illustration of receiving a gift from a friend. Maybe you don't know what the gift is, or its purpose, or anything about it. But if you trust your friend, you know the gift won't be bad for you. How much more can we trust God? If He has anything for us, whatever it is will be extremely valuable. Trust Him. He will never give us something that isn't good (see Luke 11:9-13).

I learned a long time ago that if I didn't understand a particular word or scripture, or something I believed the Lord was attempting to speak to me, I needed to find someone who understood the ways of God and the gift of His word. I'd ask questions, listen to their answers, and understand better the gift He had given me.

3. You don't know when or how, but the Word (seed sown, gift given) WILL be challenged.

...but when they have heard, Satan cometh immediately, and taketh away the word that was sown in their hearts. (Mark 4:15)

In the Parable of Parables, every example Jesus used illustrates some important principle. The devil hates the seed; the word of God. No better way to say it. He hates it because he has been on the receiving end of its sharp edge (Hebrews 4:12). He knows that if allowed to grow in a person's life, allowed to develop a root system, he'll have nothing but trouble.

The best time to remove a seed from the ground is either when it's first planted, or dead. So if the enemy can't keep someone from receiving the Word, he'll jump at every chance to remove it.

Kind of like a farmer who, every morning, walks into his field with a little trowel in his hand. Bending down, he digs up the seed he's planted, and replanted, each day for the past two weeks. Of course there won't be anything to look at other than a rootless seed. It hasn't had time to grow, to put down roots, to adjust to the soil.

The devil "encourages" us to dig up the seed and complain to God that His word isn't working. "I thought faith in God moved mountains!", we might be tempted to say. It will, if we'll let patience do what it does best; ie. - keep the seed in the ground.

I've written an entire chapter on this, called "Five Things". The devil, according to Jesus' parable of the Sower Sows the Word, uses five primary "tools" to steal, hinder, or choke the Word; or get us to abandon it altogether.

So, the Word sown into our lives WILL be challenged. Challenged by tribulations, persecutions, cares of this world, the deceitfulness of riches, and the desire for "other things". Be ready.

I have stored up Your word in my heart, that I might not sin against You. (Psalm 119:11 ESV)

The Apostle Paul wrote a simple, but powerful thought in his first letter to the Corinthians:

For a great and effective door has opened to me, and there are many adversaries. (1 Corinthians 16:9 NKJV)

Many times, when we recognize God's hand in opening doors of ministry, we become excited and ready to throw ourselves into the work.

That is, until the first sign of trouble appears.

At that point, we have a tendency to question whether or not we actually heard the Spirit's voice. We wonder if we could have been hoodwinked into believing something primarily because we wanted it to happen. And yes, that could be true.

But what PROBABLY happened is this: the adversary showed up.

Remember, he comes to steal, kill, and destroy. The quickest way for the devil to steal, kill, or destroy God's people and God's plans, is to get us sidetracked, distracted, ready to cave in due to his pressure.

With EVERY open door, you'll find an adversary close by. No exception. Count on it. Prepare for it. Arm yourselves with the mind of Christ and be ready for every good work. Study to show yourself diligent in the things of God.

No one needs to worry about trouble arriving; no, just understand your purpose and God's passion and act accordingly.

A little like Nehemiah:

Now it happened when Sanballat, Tobiah, Geshem the Arab, and the rest of our enemies heard that I had rebuilt the wall, and that there were no breaks left in it (though at that time I had not hung the doors in the gates), that Sanballat and Geshem sent to me, saying, "Come, let us meet together among the villages in the plain of Ono." But they thought to do me harm.

And I sent messengers to them, saying, "I am doing a great work, so that I cannot come down. Why should the work cease while I leave it and go down to you?"

But they sent me this message four times, and I answered them in the same manner. (Nehemiah 6:1-4 NKJV)

"I am doing a great work, with or without adversaries. I've

already committed this work to God, and that's where I will leave it."

4. What you've REALLY sown will be revealed.

And he said unto them, Is a candle brought to be put under a bushel, or under a bed? And not to be set on a candlestick? For there is nothing hid, which shall not be manifested; neither was anything kept secret, but that it should come abroad." (Mark 4:21,22)

Jesus is still talking about seeds, and the word of God. Always bear this in mind: the seed is what it is. Nothing more, nothing less. The soil won't make the seed something it isn't. You won't get a pear tree from a watermelon seed.

What you sow, you reap. Eventually. That's why it's imperative you sow the right kind of seed into your life.

The next time you sit down to read, watch TV, or do anything in which you are sowing some sort of information into your life, ask yourself these three questions:

1. What kind of harvest will the seed I'm sowing into my life bring?
2. How will it affect others?
3. Can I afford the harvest?

It really doesn't matter how intentional you are. Count on

it; whatever you sow is what you'll reap.

There have been times in my life when I've prayed for a crop failure.

It's impossible to read trashy books and expect a harvest of pure thoughts. I can't feast all day on doubt and unbelief and expect the miracle working, mountain moving faith of Almighty God to come roaring out of my spirit the moment there's a need.

Solomon wrote, "Guard your heart; for out of it flow the forces of life" (Proverbs 4:23). How does one guard their heart? Primarily, by guarding what goes into it. People will think you're weird and stuffy; "Man, you need some freedom! You're bound by legalism."

Don't let their taunts deter you from living your life with the harvest in mind. Keep your heart guarded. You will reap if you don't faint.

5. You don't need to know HOW the Word works. You only need to guard it.

If any man have ears to hear, let him hear. And he said unto them, "Take heed what ye hear: with what measure ye mete, it shall be measured to you: and unto you that hear shall more be given. For he that hath, to him shall be given: and he that hath not, from him shall be taken even that which he hath." And he said, "So is the kingdom of God, as if a man should cast seed into the ground; and should sleep, and rise night and day, and the seed should spring and grow up, he knoweth not how. For the earth bringeth forth fruit of herself; first the blade, then the ear, after that the full corn in the ear. But when the fruit is brought forth, immediately he putteth in the sickle, because the harvest is come. (Mark 4:23-29)

The Kingdom of God is like a man sowing seed into the ground; he sleeps, gets up, sleeps, gets up, sleeps some more, gets up some more. All the while the seed is working. There's nothing the man can do to make it grow quicker (outside of adding fertilizer to the soil, but that's another message). Once the blade pops through the soil into the glorious rays of the sun, it still grows according to its own timetable. Grabbing it by the stem and yanking at it won't help it grow.

No, all we can do is guard it. To guard it we first must value it. Ask yourself these questions: Is it really important? Can I live without it? How much time do I give to planting the Word into my life? Is it something I do on a daily, weekly, monthly basis, or am I content with feasting on the word of God on Christmas and Easter? Am I expecting my pastor to feed me what I need in order to become a spiritual giant, or am I "studying to show myself approved unto God, a workman that need not be ashamed, rightly dividing the word of truth" (2 Timothy 2:15)?

The seed works. The Word works! IF it's allowed to grow.

6. The most important thing to remember - "What did God say to do?"

And he said, "Whereunto shall we liken the kingdom of God? Or with what comparison shall we compare it? It is like a grain of mustard seed, which, when it is sown in the earth, is less than all the seeds that be in the earth: but when it is sown, it groweth up, and becometh greater than all herbs, and shooteth out great branches; so that the fowls of the air may lodge under the shadow of it." (Mark 4:30-32)

The Kingdom of God is a mystery, but how it operates is not. It is like a seed. A small seed. A seed that is designed, predestined if you will, to produce something of such value and importance, it can influence society and protect its citizens.

That's what God's word does! Allowed to grow in the hearts and lives of people like you and I, it will grow in such a way that will change society as it changes individuals within that society. But it requires each of us keeping this thought at the forefront of our minds - "What did God say?"

For what He said is what we're to do. And when we obey, all Heaven breaks loose! In fact, God will move Heaven and Earth if necessary to faithfully honor His word.

What did God say about sin? Purity? Youthful lusts?

What's He saying to you and I? Now? Today?

It's the patient farmer who will reap the rewards of good seed planted in a guarded heart.

Jesus, the Master Teacher, taught His disciples to pay attention to what God was saying, above all else. "Heaven and earth will pass away, but God's word never will."

So, in recapping the overall lesson Jesus taught in Mark, chapter four, I'll use a word Paul wrote in his second letter to the Corinthians.

[L]est Satan should take advantage of us; for we are not ignorant of his devices. (2 Corinthians 2:11 NKJV)

The word of God works, and is the foundation for life worth living. Allowing it to be sown into our lives isn't enough; we must be aware of the adversary's devices (or activities). Understanding and applying the principles of God's word will ensure complete victory in every stormy trial, and God's glory will be revealed through each and every situation.

Five Things

In the Parable of Parables, Jesus mentioned five basic areas in which the Word (seed) will be challenged.

Afterward, when tribulation or persecution arises for the word's sake, immediately they stumble. (Mark 4:17b NKJV)

Tribulation and persecution (for the "word's sake" or because of the word) are the first two mentioned. Tribulation isn't referring to the "Great Tribulation" of apocryphal times, but our everyday pressures, stresses, troubles, and such. Before I heard the Word about not worrying, there was no inward struggle when I worried. I just thought it was what everyone did; no one had a choice to worry or not.

But after hearing, "Don't worry about anything…", stress, pressure, etc. seemed to make me want to give up standing on the Word and begin to worry. Life appears to be hard at times; I simply MUST worry. However by doing so, the Word that was sown into my heart became unfruitful; ruined because I "dug up the seed", comparing it with my circumstances, and deciding the Word WASN'T working so I'd better start worrying.

Persecution is very similar, but the Greek word, "diogmos", indicates a more prolonged and intense struggle. It's as though the trouble is chasing you, dogging you, not letting up for an instant.

Such was the case for the Apostle Paul. Because of the abundance of revelations God had given him (2 Corinthians 12), a messenger of Satan was sent to buffet him (beat him, blow upon blow). This was NOT a messenger from God. The devil was attempting to shut down God's messenger, but God's word prevailed.

"My grace is sufficient for you", the Lord told Paul. "All you need to get through this struggle is My grace. It will give you all the strength you need to carry out My word."

Isn't that what the Lord tells us when we're in situations requiring more than we have to give?

Come boldly to the throne of GRACE...find mercy and GRACE TO HELP IN THE TIME OF NEED (Hebrews 4:16 emphasis mine).

God's grace will help us deal with tribulation and persecution. We CAN keep the Word!

The last three things the devil uses to try and keep the Word from growing into maturity are the cares of this world, the deceitfulness of riches, and the desire for other things.

...and the cares of this world, the deceitfulness of riches, and the desires for other things entering in choke the word, and it becomes unfruitful. (Mark 4:19 NKJV)

Cares of this world. So innocent looking. In fact, they are acceptable to most people, Christians included. One could wonder if Jesus meant something different.

The word "care" comes from the Greek word meaning "distractions". Distractions can be dangerous, even life threatening at times. If you're trying to cross a busy road, any distraction which causes you to focus on something other than crossing could prove to be very deadly.

When the things around us, instead of God's word, become the focus of our life, we're in trouble. Jesus said the cares, the distractions, "choke" the Word. Cares strangle and crowd out the influence and life of the Word.

Sure, one may have memorized the Word, but if distracted, that Word can be forgotten or overlooked, so it is powerless. A farmer may remember what a seed looks like. But if distracted, he could end up planting the seed deeper into the ground than it should be. Or he may not water or protect it once planted.

Scripture tells us to cast all our care upon Jesus, for He cares for us (1 Peter 5:7). Hebrews 12 instructs us to look to (fix our eyes on) Jesus. In other words, ignore the distractions and focus on Jesus and His word.

No, I didn't say to ignore the problem, or your spouse, for that matter. Ignore the DISTRACTIONS. The difference? Be responsible for that which you can tend to, and leave the results to God. Do what you KNOW to do, but do NOT try and be God.

It is very hard to have faith in God's word when we're distracted. Notice the following verses:

And they journeyed from mount Hor by the way of the Red sea, to compass the land of Edom: and the soul of the people was much discouraged because of the way. And the people spake against God, and against Moses, "Wherefore have ye brought us up out of Egypt to die in the wilderness? for there is no bread, neither is there any water; and our soul loatheth this light bread." And the Lord sent fiery serpents among the people, and they bit the people; and much people of Israel died. Therefore the people came to Moses, and said, "We have sinned, for we have spoken against the Lord, and against thee; pray unto the Lord, that he take away the serpents from us." And Moses prayed for the people. And the Lord said unto Moses, "Make thee a fiery serpent, and set it upon a pole: and it shall come to pass, that every one that is bitten, when he looketh upon it, shall live. And Moses made a serpent of brass, and put it upon a pole, and it came to pass, that if a serpent had bitten any man, when he beheld the serpent of brass, he lived. (Numbers 21:4-9)

The word of God had been given to Moses, and to the children of Israel:

And the Lord said," I have surely seen the affliction of my people which are in Egypt, and have heard their cry by reason of their taskmasters; for I know their sorrows; and I am come down to deliver them out of the hand of the Egyptians, and to bring them up out of that land unto a good land and a large, unto a land flowing with milk and honey; unto the place of the Canaanites, and the Hittites, and the Amorites, and the Perizzites, and the Hivites, and the Jebusites." (Exodus 3:7-8)

In other words, the promise of being brought IN TO the land was just as valid as being brought OUT OF the land of Egypt. If God was to bring them OUT, He was also going to bring them IN.

But along the way the people of God FORGOT the promises by allowing themselves to be distracted by all the circumstances and situations in the wilderness. They complained about the lack of water, lack of meat, and Moses' leadership. AND they complained about the manna from heaven; God's miraculous provision.

Their complaining did nothing but cause more problems.

The cares of their lives coaxed them into complaining

about the bread from heaven. Wow.

The wages of sin is death (Romans 6:23), and sure enough, their complaining was as sinful as the time they manipulated Aaron into making the golden calf.

So as the fiery serpents invaded the camp, the people all of a sudden had a change of heart.

"Moses! Help us! Pray for us!"

And Moses prayed for them.

The Lord's answer seems strange. To those so easily distracted with the cares of the world, the remedy for their ills seemed a bit impossible; if not just a bit ridiculous.

"Make a bronze image of a serpent; the kind of serpent that has invaded your lives. Set it upon a pole, raising it high enough for everyone to see. Then, whoever has been bitten by a serpent and looks upon the pole will be healed."

Amazing.

Seems simple enough, doesn't it? Again, I refer you to John 3:14-17. Also, Paul wrote, *"[Jesus] became sin, Who knew no sin, that we could become the righteousness of God in Christ" (2 Corinthians 5:21)*.

But stop and consider the situation. There were snakes slithering everywhere. In their tents, in their sleeping bags, around their feet and the feet of their animals. Talk about distractions.

The Lord's word, "Whoever looks shall live", depicts much more than a casual glance. The Amplified Translation reads this way:

...when he looked to the serpent of bronze (attentively, expectantly, with a steady and absorbing gaze), he lived. (Numbers 21:9 Amplified)

"Attentively, expectantly, with a steady and absorbing gaze."

That's what brought healing to the camp. Ignoring the distractions, not the problem. The problem WASN'T the snakes. The problem was their rebellious complaining.

Proverbs 4:20-22 tells us to "...attend and submit to" the sayings of the Lord. Though the cares of this life have a tendency to turn our heads away from God's instructions, with the help of the Holy Spirit we can ignore the distractions and focus our attention on "thus saith the Lord."

Jesus also mentioned the deceitfulness of riches as something the enemy uses to choke the Word so it doesn't bear the kind of fruit it's designed to produce.

The word "deceitful" means "to lie, to cheat, to delude". Someone who is deceitful never reveals their true motive. They won't tell you the whole story, or the whole cost.

Riches CAN come in handy. God isn't against His kids having them. But it's a terrible thing when riches become the focus of one's trust.

Riches can be a valuable tool, but a horrible master.

One's bank account should never be the determining factor of whether or not to obey God. Jesus didn't tell the devil that man lives according to their net worth. No. Man lives, REALLY lives, by the Word that proceeds from the mouth of God.

Paul wrote to Timothy, addressing the subject of riches, in 1 Timothy 6: 17-19:

Charge them that are rich in this world, that they be not high-minded, nor trust in uncertain riches, but in the living God, who giveth us richly all things to enjoy; that they do good, that they be rich in good works, ready to distribute, willing to communicate; laying up in store for themselves a good foundation against the time to come, that they may lay hold on eternal life. (1 Timothy 6:17-19)

The word "high-minded" means "arrogant, lofty in mind". Pleased with self's accomplishments, and forgetting it is God Who gives people the power to get wealth

(Deuteronomy 8:18). The "I've got to get more and more" spirit will plug one's spiritual ears and keep the Word from producing fruit. However, those who trust in the living God as their source can be rich in good works and always ready to help someone in need.

There's a phrase I heard a long time ago; I haven't a clue as to who the author is. But it goes something like this. "A lot of people have this attitude where money is concerned: they get all they can, can all they get, and then sit on their can."

Think about it. The meaning will come to you.

It's a way of describing those who have become carried away with the deceitfulness of riches.

Deceitful?

Yes.

Deceitful.

Because most of life's important things cannot be purchased, protected, or proliferated with money.

One more thing Jesus added to the choking list: the desire for other things. It means to "set the heart upon" things, specifically forbidden things. Things other than those mentioned by the Lord as what we should be pursuing.

For instance, the Lord told Adam, "You may surely eat of every tree of the garden, but of the tree of the knowledge of good and evil, you shall not eat" (Genesis 2:16,17). They could eat of EVERY TREE, including the TREE OF LIFE, with only ONE EXCEPTION. That exception was what got them into trouble.

The lust for other things choked the word God had given Adam.

And it affects you and I the same way.

THE STORMY TEST

I dislike tests. No, I hate tests.

But there is no graduating without them.

Tests reveal what a person has learned.

Tests are a normal part of living, so we might as well get used to it.

Some people believe God tests us to find out how we'll react to a certain situation. I'm more inclined to believe we go through tests to help us understand how little we really know. But whatever the reason, count on it. Tests are a part of life.

Every teacher gives tests. Jesus is no different. When He taught the disciples the truths recorded in the fourth chapter of Mark, He even told them to make sure they were prepared for the test. Now, He said it a bit differently than a teacher would say it today, "OK, class. Close your books, clear your desk of everything except a pencil and a blank sheet of paper". No, He said, "The sower sows the Word. And Satan comes immediately to steal the Word." He then went on to describe the five primary ways that the devil uses to steal the Word.

What you and I have believed and received (or think we have), will be challenged.

Tested.

Just like our faith is challenged. Tested. Tried as gold is tried. In other words, the heat is applied and the fake gold, the dirt and junk that's mixed in with faith rises to the surface.

Why would the Lord want faith tested with heat (or pressure)? So we can understand it for what it really is, and take necessary action to remove that which isn't approved by the Lord.

Hebrews 11:6 reads, "Without faith it is impossible to please Him...". It's not what WE say is faith; it's what HE says after the paper is graded.

Wherein ye greatly rejoice, though now for a season, if need be, ye are in heaviness through manifold temptations: that the trial of your faith, being much more precious than of gold that perisheth, though it be tried with fire, might be found unto praise and honour and glory at the appearing of Jesus Christ: (1 Peter 1:6-7)

The appearing of Jesus Christ. When He is revealed in and through our lives.

God is glorified when His will is done on earth. He's glorified when people believe Him and stand on His word even in the midst of trying situations; simply because He said so.

It's what pleases Him.

So let's see what happens in Mark's gospel AFTER Jesus ends the training seminar. I'll use Mark 4:35-41 as my text.

But first I want you to notice something. The SAME day Jesus taught His guys is the SAME day He gave them a pop quiz. The SAME day they were challenged.

And the same day, when the even was come, he saith unto them, "Let us pass over unto the other side." (Mark 4:35)

I think I'd better clear something up. I say that Jesus gave them a pop quiz. Then I mention the devil tries to steal the Word, or challenge it. But I am NOT saying Jesus and the devil are tag-teaming; they are NOT in cahoots with one another. They do NOT work together. Light and darkness have NO communion, whatsoever. Righteousness and unrighteousness do not have the same goals.

The devil ONLY wants to steal, kill, and destroy. He's after control, and he thinks he's due our worship. Jesus on the other hand, came to bring us life and DESTROY the works of the devil. The devil sees every test as an opportunity to tempt, to lure us away from God's living word. Jesus knows the test will reveal the true condition of our heart.

The Teacher, on the same day He taught, told His class to get in their boat and go to the other side of the lake. He spoke to them eight words. Just eight common words. But those words carried with them all the power of Heaven and Earth.

Remember what Jesus had taught them? Here's a quick reminder:

As Jesus and His disciples got into the boat, He told them what He wanted to do. He revealed to them His will. "Let us pass over to the other side."

The verse Jesus quoted to the devil, in Matthew 4:4, "Man shall not live by bread alone, but by every word that proceeds from the mouth of God", is a critical verse to know, believe, and practice when it comes to guarding the word in one's heart.

When Jesus said, "Let us pass over to the other side", the

faith necessary to make it to the other side was wrapped up in those spoken words. Faith comes by hearing the word of God (Romans 10:17), right? Faith is possible where the will of God is known. When a person hears, believes, and receives the word of God, faith comes.

Faith. The powerful force capable of moving mountains, raising the dead, healing the sick, and mending broken marriages.

And a shield against every fiery dart of the wicked one; including one that arrives as a storm in the middle of the night.

"Let us pass over to the other side." Jesus never told them the reason for the journey. Faith in God's word isn't about the future, or the reason why He said what He did.

True, on the other side of the sea was a mad, demon-possessed man just begging to be set free. There were hundreds of townspeople who would hear the gospel of the Kingdom through a man set free by the power of God. But the disciples didn't know all that when Jesus gave them His word, "Let us pass over to the other side."

The Word was enough to get them to the other side. Even if the boat had been lost, the Lord would have found a way to get to the other side. The promises of God are yes and amen (2 Corinthians 1:20).

There was NOTHING in His words that day that

promised a storm-free trip. In fact, Psalm 91 reads, "I will be with him in trouble, to deliver him...".

Psalm 46 has more faith-filled promises:

God is our refuge and strength, a very present help in trouble. Therefore will not we fear, though the earth be removed, and though the mountains be carried into the midst of the sea; though the waters thereof roar and be troubled, though the mountains shake with the swelling thereof. Selah. (Psalms 46:1-3)

A very PRESENT help IN trouble. Hallelujah!

The word of God is enough to get you and I to the other side as well. We can go through ANYTHING, if we're obeying and believing the word of God.

As they began their journey to the other side, the tired Teacher found Himself a pillow to rest upon. He wasn't concerned at all about the possibility of encountering a storm. He had heard from His Father; and He would make it to the other side.

(Remember, Jesus said, "I only do what I see My Father do.")

But in the middle of the trip, Jesus was awakened by a group of fear-filled sailors.

And he was in the hinder part of the ship, asleep on a

pillow: and they awake him, and say unto him, "Master, carest thou not that we perish?" (Mark 4:38)

The back of the boat is where Jesus was sleeping. If you've ever had the unfortunate experience of standing in a boat that was sinking, you'll know that's where the most water was. But soggy shoes, a flooded boat, or even a giant squid can't keep you from witnessing the Glory of God - if you'll stay with what God told you to do.

"Don't you care?", the disciples asked their Teacher. Really? Is that the question we should ask the Lord in times of trouble? Hasn't He shown His concern over and over? Yes. He has!

Care. Distractions. "Aren't You distracted by this storm, Jesus? Don't You realize we're not in the shallow part of the sea? We won't make it if this keeps up. We'll never live to see the other side."

What were they armed with? What had they sown into their lives? Like us, they were well aware of how bad things can get. They knew, because they had witnessed storms before.

But they had something they didn't have before. They had God's will. "Let us pass over to the other side." It was their anchor, their hope and foundation for faith, and they had the Lord WITH them.

EVERY TIME you and I choose to obey God's word, He

comes alongside to see us through. Whether we are standing on His promises against temptations, worry, fear, or anything else, He is WITH US.

When Jesus was fully awake, He rebuked the wind and the waves. He said, "Peace, be still." And the sea and waves obeyed Him. Just like that.

I've read that verse time and time again, and have pictured Jesus standing tall in the boat, facing the wind, hair blowing behind Him, arm pointed to the sky, screaming, "PEACE, BE STILL!!!" And I've tried doing that in the midst of some of my tests and trials.

But screaming has never worked for me, and I don't believe that's what Jesus did either. The word, "said", simply refers to something spoken OR WRITTEN. Faith isn't rooted in the lungs; it's connected to the heart. We believe with our heart and say, declare, confess, with our mouths.

I'm NOT saying there's never a time to shout. If you want to shout, then shout. But the power isn't in the volume. Unless of course God tells you to shout. Then by all means SHOUT!

"Teacher, don't You care?" Yes He did and yes He does.

Did you notice what Jesus did AFTER He rebuked the wind and waves? He rebuked His class. "Why didn't you believe?" Now why would He ask such a thing?

Because He had just taught them about receiving the word of God, keeping it planted, guarding it against things that would choke it and make it unfruitful. And then He planted a word into their heart when He said, "Let us pass over to the other side."

I use this passage not to poke fun at anyone, but to show us (myself included) just how easy it is to pass or fail a test. The winning difference? Keeping the Word in our heart to such a degree it's the only thing that matters.

That's what I call being "armed with the mind of Christ".

Yes, thank God Jesus was in the boat and didn't let them drown. He's helped me out of more jams and jellies than I can remember, that's for sure.

But He really wants us to grow in Him, and live a life that brings Glory to Him in everything we do. "Thy Kingdom come, Thy will be done, in earth as it is in Heaven!"

Amen.

Did you happen to notice how each thing Jesus taught His class was tested?

1. The Word makes the winning difference. They let it fall overboard.
2. You must receive and hold on to the Word. Regardless.
3. The Word was challenged, to keep them from doing God's will.

4. What was sown in their heart (through the years) was revealed. HELP!
5. They didn't protect the Word; they acted as though it wasn't working.
6. Distractions took their focus from God's word; their gaze was fixed on their trouble.

Now let's see if any of these principles can be found in chapters five and six. Remember, we are discussing the importance of arming ourselves with the mind of Christ, for "he who has suffered in the flesh has ceased from sin...". Ceased from doing things contrary to the will of God. Ceased from yielding to the deceptive and ultimately deplorable schemes of the devil.

ADDITIONAL TRAINING AND TESTS

I'll begin this chapter with a quick review.

Jesus taught His disciples a Parable of Parables. "Understand this parable", He said, "and you will have the key to all the rest."

The sower sowing the Word is the key revelation of how the Kingdom of God operates, and how God's will is accomplished in the earth. Remember the prayer Jesus told us to pray:

"Thy Kingdom come, Thy will be done; in earth as it is in Heaven."

God's word is His will. His command is ours to obey. Read what King David thought about the Word, as he was inspired by the Holy Spirit to write many, many years ago:

The law of the Lord is perfect, converting the soul; the testimony of the Lord is sure, making wise the simple; the statutes of the Lord are right, rejoicing the heart; the commandment of the Lord is pure, enlightening the eyes; the fear of the Lord is clean, enduring forever; the judgments of the Lord are true and righteous altogether. More to be desired are they than gold, yea, than much fine gold; sweeter also than honey and the honeycomb. Moreover by them Your servant is warned, and in keeping them there is great reward. (Psalms 19:7-11 NKJV)

Jesus' parable in Mark's gospel can be summarized in this manner:

1. The Word makes all the difference between winning or losing.
2. You MUST receive AND hold on to the Word.
3. You don't know when or how, but the Word (seed sown, gift given) WILL be challenged.
4. What you've REALLY sown will be revealed.
5. You don't need to know HOW the Word works. You only need to guard it.
6. The most important thing to remember - "What did God say to do?"

Reading through the fifth and sixth chapters of Mark (while the lessons taught by the Teacher are still fresh in the students' minds), notice Jesus took His class on a field trip. He taught them, not only by the words He spoke, but by using a method many refer to as "teaching by precept and example".

And they came over unto the other side of the sea, into the country of the Gadarenes. And when he was come out of the ship, immediately there met him out of the tombs a man with an unclean spirit... (Mark 5:1-2)

Jesus and His disciples weathered the storm so they could come face to face with a demon-possessed madman. I can picture the twelve talking among themselves, murmuring something akin to the complaining Israelites in the wilderness. "We were probably better off drowning in the sea than facing this nut!"

The boat ride was part of God's will; for the Lord cared for the madman. In fact, there isn't a soul living on the face of this planet that doesn't have a special place in God's heart. But at the risk of sounding simple and redundant, God's will doesn't automatically mean smooth sailing.

Here they were, the freshman class of Jesus followers, watching Him as He stepped out of the boat and into the path of a man who was naked as a jaybird.

Mark didn't write anything about what the disciples were thinking while Jesus and the demoniac were having dialogue. However, I'm positive each of them had their eyes glued on what was taking place. And whether they knew it or not, they were soon to be tested on what they were learning. Jesus told them so during their last teaching session. What could they have learned by watching Jesus and the madman?

First of all, they learned compassion. Ministry isn't only about imparting information to someone. It's not just pulpit duty. Ministry is serving others. Compassion is a foundation of ministry. Compassion not only sees a need ("Isn't that a shame?"), but seeks to meet the need using whatever means are available.

Somewhat like Peter's words to the lame man in Acts 3: "I'm not loaded with silver and gold. But THIS is what I have; in the Name of Jesus rise up and walk."

They learned compassion can be messy business. Up close and personal. Maybe a little risky. And time consuming. There isn't always a quick fix available.

Another thing they saw, and would have tested throughout their lives, is that not everyone agrees with you. Some people think you're weird; maybe nuttier than the one you're attempting to help.

Some folks really don't appreciate having their world turned upside down with change. Once they have gotten used to someone acting a certain way, well, don't change it. Especially if it's going to cost the community a couple thousand hogs! Way over the top!

Above all, the class witnessed the God of Heaven touching a man society had given up on. Almighty God knew what was needed to set him free. And all the disciples needed to do was stand on His word - "Let us pass over to the other side".

As the Teacher and His pupils returned to the boat and prepared to sail back to the other side, it wouldn't surprise me if they were just a little bit excited. "Here we go again, guys. But we're ready for the storm. Bring it on. And bring on another demon-possessed dude. Let's show everyone what WE can do."

Sorry guys, no storm this time. And no madman. But keep watching. Class is still in session.

And when Jesus was passed over again by ship unto the other side, much people gathered unto him: and he was nigh unto the sea. And, behold, there cometh one of the rulers of the synagogue, Jairus by name; and when he saw him, he fell at his feet, and besought him greatly, saying, "My little daughter lieth at the point of death: I pray thee, come and lay thy hands on her, that she may be healed; and she shall live." And Jesus went with him; and much people followed him, and thronged him. (Mark 5:21-24)

A new phase of training was about to begin. Lessons you and I need to learn as well, if we are to "arm ourselves"; if we are to be ready in season, and out of season.

A man named Jairus came bursting through the crowd, attempting to get Jesus' attention. It's what people do when they are desperate. Desperate people aren't always well behaved. They don't always think straight. They may be downright rude and obnoxious.

But that's who Jesus came for. And it's to those kinds of people we are sent.

Jesus would leave a crowd to help one person. Would you? Would I? Are YOU armed with the mind of Christ? Is one just as important as the ninety nine?

Jesus met with Jairus at his point of faith. A centurion once told Jesus, "Just speak the word and my servant will be healed." Jesus didn't try and talk the synagogue ruler into believing just like the centurion. He met him where he was.

It's a good thing for us to understand the power of God may vary at times. God doesn't work the same way each and every time. "According to your faith..." is powerful enough to make a difference. Meeting people at their level of faith, what they are capable of believing, is what Jesus taught His disciples; and it's what He is teaching us.

And a certain woman, which had an issue of blood twelve years, and had suffered many things of many physicians, and had spent all that she had, and was nothing bettered, but rather grew worse, when she had heard of Jesus, came in the press behind, and touched his garment... And he looked round about to see her that had done this thing. But the woman fearing and trembling, knowing what was done in her, came and fell down before him, and told him all the truth. And he said unto her, "Daughter, thy faith hath made thee whole; go in peace, and be whole of thy plague." (Mark 5:25-34)

Here was a passionate woman interrupting something Jesus was trying to do. The woman stopped the healing/salvation procession, and yet Jesus didn't seem to mind.

Faith is NOW. Right now! *"Now faith is the substance of things hoped for; the evidence of things not yet seen" (Hebrews 11:1).* When faith comes alive in someone's heart, they can't be, won't be, stopped for anything. Be ready to move with God, Who will move according to someone's faith.

While he yet spake, there came from the ruler of the synagogue's house certain which said, "Thy daughter is dead: why troublest thou the Master any further?" As soon as Jesus heard the word that was spoken, he saith unto the ruler of the synagogue, "Be not afraid, only believe..." (Mark 5:35-42)

I believe Peter remembered this lesson when he was called to Joppa to raise a woman from the dead (Acts 9). Not everyone will unite as one in faith. That's alright. Don't try and force the issue. Hear God's instructions, join with those whose eyes are fixed on Jesus, and continue with the assignment of faith.

Jesus probably noticed Jairus' countenance fall when he

heard the bad news. But Jesus stayed with the man and his faith, as we are to do when confronted with troublesome news. Bad news isn't necessarily the final word. Bad news may be nothing more than a device of the devil to get us to move off our dogged stance on God's word.

We'd best stay with what is designed to last.

And he went out from thence, and came into his own country; and his disciples follow him. And when the sabbath day was come, he began to teach in the synagogue: and many hearing him were astonished, saying, "From whence hath this man these things? And what wisdom is this which is given unto him, that even such mighty works are wrought by his hands? Is not this the carpenter, the son of Mary, the brother of James, and Joses, and of Juda, and Simon? And are not his sisters here with us?" And they were offended at him. But Jesus said unto them, "A prophet is not without honour, but in his own country, and among his own kin, and in his own house." And he could there do no mighty work, save that he laid his hands upon a few sick folk, and healed them. And he marvelled because of their unbelief. And he went round about the villages, teaching. (Mark 6:1-6)

Three things stand out to me here. First, success isn't measured by someone's approval or disapproval. Second, it may be a surprise to see who is offended and who isn't. Third, the way to try and overcome unbelief is by teaching truth.

All three lessons were learned by the disciples; later called apostles. Peter himself stood in front of the religious council and told them, "We need to obey God, not you." Jerusalem was offended when Paul was converted and began preaching about Jesus. In fact, people conspired to kill Paul, as those in Nazareth tried to kill Jesus (Luke 4). And the disciples went everywhere (Acts 8) preaching the Word.

Remember the words of Jesus: "Go into all the world and make disciples..." Disciples are not born, they are made.

And he called unto him the twelve, and began to send them forth by two and two; and gave them power over unclean spirits; and commanded them that they should take nothing for their journey, save a staff only; no scrip, no bread, no money in their purse; but be shod with sandals; and not put on two coats. And he said unto them, "In what place soever ye enter into an house, there abide till ye depart from that place. And whosoever shall not receive you, nor hear you, when ye depart thence, shake off the dust under your feet for a testimony against them. Verily I say unto you, It shall be more tolerable for Sodom and Gomorrha in the day of judgment, than for that city." And they went out, and preached that men should repent. And they cast out many devils, and anointed with oil many that were sick, and healed them. (Mark 6:7-13)

Jesus sent His students out to do the very thing He did - bring the Kingdom of God to the multitudes. As God "anointed Jesus with the Holy Ghost and power", so He anointed Jesus' students. They went about "doing good, and healing all who were oppressed by the devil". God was with them; with them in the learning stage, and with them during the testing part. All they needed to do was obey Jesus' words and imitate all they had seen Him do.

A disciple is not above his teacher, nor a servant above his master. It is enough for a disciple that he be like his teacher, and a servant like his master... (Matthew 10:24-25 NKJV)

Remember our foundational scriptures? "...As Christ has suffered in the flesh for us, so arm yourselves with the same mind...", 1 Peter 4:1,2. Disciples don't just train to be victorious. They don't just talk about it, patting each other on the back for memorizing a ton of scripture. No, disciples of Jesus keep learning, practicing, and imitating Jesus until they look and act exactly like their Master.

The disciple of Jesus is armed and ready to do the will of God.

And the apostles gathered themselves together unto Jesus, and told him all things, both what they had done, and what they had taught. And he said unto them, "Come ye yourselves apart into a desert place, and rest a while"; for there were many coming and going, and they had no leisure so much as to eat. And they departed into a desert place by ship privately. And the people saw them departing, and many knew him, and ran afoot thither out of all cities, and outwent them, and came together unto him. And Jesus, when he came out, saw much people, and was moved with compassion toward them, because they were as sheep not having a shepherd: and he began to teach them many things. And when the day was now far spent, his disciples came unto him, and said, "This is a desert place, and now the time is far passed: send them away, that they may go into the country round about, and into the villages, and buy themselves bread: for they have nothing to eat." He answered and said unto them, "Give ye them to eat." And they say unto him, "Shall we go and buy two hundred pennyworth of bread, and give them to eat?" He saith unto them, "How many loaves have ye? Go and see." And when they knew, they say, "Five, and two fishes." And he commanded them to make all sit down by companies upon the green grass...(Mark 6:30-45)

Just because a disciple of Jesus has had some wonderful, exciting experiences as they've obeyed the Lord, they have not arrived at the point of no longer needing additional schooling. Note the above passage. Jesus' students had just returned from their ministry trip, all excited and full of testimonies. Jesus' response? "Let's get away from everything for a bit and rest."

But they couldn't rest. Too many people were coming and going. Too many people with needs and wants. Too many folks hungry for something only Jesus or His disciples could give them.

Did you catch that? Jesus told His team, "You give them something to eat." "Impossible", is what they thought. But God doesn't put us through training to do ordinary things; He wants us to do EXTRAORDINARY things! Things we can't do without trusting Him for the necessary power and ability.

Training continues, even at times when we least expect it.

And when he had sent them away, he departed into a mountain to pray. And when even was come, the ship was in the midst of the sea, and he alone on the land. And he saw them toiling in rowing; for the wind was contrary unto them: and about the fourth watch of the night he cometh unto them, walking upon the sea, and would have passed by them. But when they saw him walking upon the sea, they supposed it had been a spirit, and cried out: for they all saw him, and were troubled. And immediately he talked with them, and saith unto them, "Be of good cheer: it is I; be not afraid." And he went up unto them into the ship; and the wind ceased: and they were sore amazed in themselves beyond measure, and wondered. For they considered not the miracle of the loaves: for their heart was hardened... And whithersoever he entered, into villages, or cities, or country, they laid the sick in the streets, and besought him that they might touch if it were but the border of his garment: and as many as touched him were made whole. (Mark 6:46-56)

Almost a repeat of the first sea cruise test, the disciples were toiling in rowing, struggling to get to the other side. As He approached His students, it seems as though He had planned to let them work at it until they figured out what was wrong. Yet, when they saw Him and He noticed they were troubled, He calmed their fears and entered the boat.

But here's where we really need to be on guard. The disciples were "sore amazed" and wondered. Why? Hadn't they witnessed plenty of signs and wonders performed by Jesus? Hadn't they themselves performed miracles as they went forth in His Name?

Yes, they had.

So what was wrong? They allowed their hearts to become hardened. They didn't consider what He'd done or said in the past.

Even disciples can become hard hearted or faithless, when they need a miracle. But that's why Jesus continually tries to teach us; teaching us by His words and His actions. And it's how we grow more and more into His likeness.

Further training is always on the docket for anyone who truly desires to be a disciple of Jesus. To be armed with the same mind as Christ, is to expect and welcome opportunities to put into practice what we've learned from Jesus.

By doing so we will be "thoroughly equipped for every good work", 2 Timothy 3:17.

Prepare The Way Of The Lord

There is a reason why we are still living here, and why we're not transported to Heaven to be with Jesus immediately after experiencing the New Birth.

It's true, Paul said "to depart and be with Christ is far better" than just hanging around planet earth. Yes, and I'm convinced Heaven has just about anything a person could ever want.

Just about?

There's one thing Heaven cannot offer the child of God. I'm sure you're wondering what I'm referring to, so I'll explain myself.

The one thing Heaven cannot offer the child of God is someone who still needs to witness a demonstration of the Kingdom of God. There isn't anyone in Heaven who hasn't been born again.

Everyone in Heaven has heard the Good News. They've heard it, embraced it, and received Jesus as the Lord of their life.

Everyone in Heaven is full of the Holy Spirit, enjoys complete and total health, and fully trusts in the Son Who lights the Eternal City.

And there's not a tear among them.

That's why we're still here, living in this strange and ungodly world.

This is where we're needed.

On earth, not in Heaven. Of course, I'm looking forward to the day when my job is finished and I'm called home to be with Christ. But in the meantime, I must remain faithful to His calling and stay armed for His glory.

When the Decapolis Demoniac became the Decapolis Disciple, he desired to get in the boat with Jesus and the others. But the Lord wasn't gathering a bunch of guys for a men's fellowship breakfast, or even a men's choir.

...Jesus did not permit him, but said to him, "Go home to your friends, and tell them what great things the Lord has done for you, and how He has had compassion on you." And he departed and began to proclaim in

Decapolis all that Jesus had done for him; and all marveled. (Mark 5:19-20 NKJV)

The Lord is attempting to make disciples out of us. People armed with the mind of Christ, not only for our sakes, but for those who haven't taken the plunge into eternal life. A disciple is one who doesn't just hang out, but imitates his Master; the One Who came to seek and save the lost.

Paul told the Philippian believers that while he would rather leave this life and be with Jesus, he knew they needed him more than Heaven did. How's that for a healthy, Christ-like attitude?

The prophet Isaiah wrote, *"Prepare the way of the Lord; make straight in the desert a highway for our God" (Isaiah 40:3)*, thus describing one facet of Jesus' earthly ministry.

It also describes the ministry of each and every disciple. Each follower of Jesus Christ.

Clear the path. Make it possible for people to find their way to the Lord, and the Lord to find His way into their lives. Remove the obstacles, present your proof. Declare the word of the Lord, which endures forever. Broadcast far and wide, 'Behold your God!' (Isaiah 40:3-9 paraphrased)

Arming our minds with the testimony of Jesus is one powerful way to prepare the way of the Lord.

Jesus entered into the desert battle with the word of God AND the word of His testimony. The woman at the well (John 4) entered into her village with the testimony of her encounter with Jesus, thus preparing the way for many others to connect with the Lord.

And the Decapolis Disciple prepared the way of the Lord when he obeyed Jesus' words, and went throughout the region armed with the testimony of God's goodness and power.

And they overcame him by the blood of the Lamb, and by the word of their testimony; and they loved not their lives unto the death. (Revelation 12:11)

Overcoming the enemy is necessary if we're to clear the highway for our God. Submitting ourselves to the authority of Jesus, recognizing and utilizing the testimony of His work in us, and placing our very lives in His hand, is something the devil has no countermeasure for. But we must arm ourselves with the same mind as Christ.

With Jesus it was God's confirmation "You are my beloved Son, in Whom I am well pleased." He had stated, "I have come to do Your will", and He did.

With the woman at the well, as she left Jesus and went into town, she said, "Come see a Man Who told me everything about me. Is not this the Christ?" They believed because of her testimony and word. She prepared a way for her God.

The Decapolis Disciple simply heard Jesus say, "Go home, and tell your friends and family what the Lord did for you." He obeyed, and the next time Jesus was in the area the people were ready to meet with God!

And again, departing from the coasts of Tyre and Sidon, he came unto the sea of Galilee, through the midst of the coasts of Decapolis. (Mark 7:31)

Decapolis. Ten cities. A region on the east side of the Sea of Galilee. The ex-madman's stomping grounds. A place prepared for the way of the Lord. Through the testimony of the delivered one and the power of the Lord, the deaf could hear and the dumb could speak.

People armed with nothing more than the knowledge of what Jesus did for them cleared the pathway for a visitation of God.

What has Jesus done for you? You haven't forgotten, have you? Remember, it is written of you in the Volume of the Book.

Many things can hinder people from meeting with Jesus face to face. For example, in Luke chapter five there's the story of the paralytic and his four friends. The friends knew somehow if they could just get their paralyzed friend to Jesus everything would be fine.

But a number of things blocked the way to the Lord. They knew where He was but they couldn't get close. Crowds, walls, rude and outspoken people; so close and yet so far away.

However, they FOUND a way. Climbing up on the roof of the house where Jesus was speaking, and lifting their friend with them, they tore a hole in the roof big enough for them to lower the paralytic and his cot until he and Jesus were face to face. "Arise, take up your bed and walk!"

A miracle, not only because Jesus was anointed with the Holy Spirit and power, but because four ordinary men armed themselves with faith. Faith that would not let go of their hope or the Lord's promise.

It's what people need today. Friends armed with the same mind as Christ. People who have settled in their heart Who it is they're living for, and dying for, if necessary. People who no longer live their lives for the lust and dictates of their flesh, but for the will and Glory of God.

Come on people, make His paths straight.

Finishing Well

What believer doesn't want to hear Jesus say, "Well done, good and faithful servant. Enter into the joy of the Lord"?

I know of none.

Of all the people I know who proclaim Christ Jesus as their Lord and Savior, not one of them wants to miss out on a heavenly eternity.

Then why are so many struggling to finish their life in a manner that pleases the Lord?

Why are some pastors throwing in the towel of servanthood, and running after a lifestyle of craziness and selfishness?

Why have people left their spouses, families, and friends to pursue a relationship with "someone who really cares, who knows how to listen, and identifies with me"?

Beginning well doesn't automatically mean finishing well.

We must arm ourselves with the mind of Christ. A person who is ARMED WELL will FINISH WELL.

Paul's thorn, mentioned in 2 Corinthians 12, almost pushed him into the "I'm tired of fighting this thing" waters of despair. Three times he sought God about his situation. And God gave him something he could use to arm himself.

The grace of God.

It's what Jesus used to enable Himself to go to the cross as our sacrificial lamb.

...that he (Jesus) by the grace of God should taste death for every man. (Hebrews 2:9)

Paul armed himself with the mind of Jesus and was able to say, "I take pleasure in infirmities and distresses...for Christ's sake...for when I'm weak, then I'm strong."

And at the end of his life his testimony was:

I have fought a good fight, I have finished my course, I have kept the faith: (2 Timothy 4:7)

A person who is ARMED WELL will FINISH WELL.

Philip was in the midst of a city-wide revival when the Lord gave him some unexpected directions. "Arise and go to a place south of Jerusalem, to the Gaza road."

"Really, Lord? We're having a powerful time here, You know. The whole city is filled with joy as people are getting saved, filled with the Holy Spirit, and delivered from demons and disease. Leave now? We've finally got the offerings up to a respectable level. Leave now?"

But he was armed with the mind of Christ.

Jesus left His glorious home, from where He ruled the universe, to live in this filthy, crazy world. He did it because of what He said: "I have come to do Your will, O God."

Philip heard the Spirit speak, and armed with the mind of Christ, "arose and went."

And that's how the gospel message found its way into Ethiopia. See Acts 8.

Peter had a preoccupation with greatness, and liked to fit in with different crowds. Remember when he betrayed Jesus three times that fateful night? Sure, that was before he was saved and filled with the Holy Spirit.

But AFTERWARD, he still had a problem from time to time. See Galatians 2:11,12.

Remember, Peter is the apostle who wrote the letter to us explaining our need to arm ourselves. So somewhere along the way, his preoccupation with greatness, fitting in with the crowds, and having to know other people's business, gave way to the mind of Christ.

For Peter's own words, in 1 Peter 5, are: "...I who am a fellow elder and a witness of the sufferings of Christ, and also a partaker of the glory that will be revealed..."(verse 1), demonstrate a humility in Peter not seen in prior passages. And in his second letter he says, "...to those who have obtained like precious faith..."; in other words, faith just as powerful and personal as the faith I have.

Peter. Armed with the mind of Christ. Finishing well.

You and I have been ordained by God to finish well. It's in our DNA. It's part of being a new creation in Christ. Finishing well is the will of God.

We understand that the sin issue has been dealt a final, once and for all, permanent death blow through the death, burial, and resurrection of Jesus Christ. All who put their trust in Him are recreated into the image of God's Son.

Now we must arm ourselves with the mind of Christ; for those who do cease from sin and please God in everything they do.

To help us arm ourselves, God has a number of examples

of what He's doing in us, and what He's already DONE for us - in the Volume of the Book. We can do all things, because we do what Christ desires and empowers us to do.

We are armed for battle by the Prince of Peace. We are armed to protect ourselves and others as our mind is renewed by the word of God. We recognize there are things dispatched by the evil one, designed to either steal the Word or choke it from our lives. But we lock it into our heart, keep it on the tip of our tongue, and prepare for every test and challenge.

We are armed. We will finish well.

And while we're still here on earth, armed with the mind of Christ, we will prepare the way of the Lord. The Glory of God will be revealed through our lives, and others will hear and be glad that "Our God Reigns!"

Amen.

So be it!

Jan Grace

Other books by Jan Grace:

- The Power Of Encouragement
- Boot Camp - Basic Training For The Believer
- Picked Off - The Target Is You
- American Idols
- How To Get The Most Out Of Your Pastor
- Breaking The Spirit Of Poverty (With...Generosity)
- A Steady Stream (Daily Devotional)

Available at Amazon.com

Made in the USA
San Bernardino, CA
01 October 2015